EXPLORING THE STATES

Montana

THE TREASURE STATE

by Emily Rose Oachs

BELLWETHER MEDIA • MINNEAPOLIS, MN

Note to Librarians, Teachers, and Parents:

Blastoff! Readers are carefully developed by literacy experts and combine standards-based content with developmentally appropriate text.

Level 1 provides the most support through repetition of high-frequency words, light text, predictable sentence patterns, and strong visual support.

Level 2 offers early readers a bit more challenge through varied simple sentences, increased text load, and less repetition of high-frequency words.

Level 3 advances early-fluent readers toward fluency through increased text and concept load, less reliance on visuals, longer sentences, and more literary language.

Level 4 builds reading stamina by providing more text per page, increased use of punctuation, greater variation in sentence patterns, and increasingly challenging vocabulary.

Level 5 encourages children to move from "learning to read" to "reading to learn" by providing even more text, varied writing styles, and less familiar topics.

Whichever book is right for your reader, Blastoff! Readers are the perfect books to build confidence and encourage a love of reading that will last a lifetime!

This edition first published in 2014 by Bellwether Media, Inc.

No part of this publication may be reproduced in whole or in part without written permission of the publisher.
For information regarding permission, write to Bellwether Media, Inc., Attention: Permissions Department,
5357 Penn Avenue South, Minneapolis, MN 55419.

Library of Congress Cataloging-in-Publication Data

Oachs, Emily Rose.
 Montana / by Emily Rose Oachs.
   pages cm. – (Blastoff! readers. Exploring the states)
 Includes bibliographical references and index.
 Summary: "Developed by literacy experts for students in grades three through seven, this book introduces young readers
to the geography and culture of Montana"–Provided by publisher.
 ISBN 978-1-62617-025-4 (hardcover : alk. paper)
 1. Montana–Juvenile literature. I. Title.
 F731.3.O34 2014
 978.6–dc23
                                                                    2013009006

Printed in the United States of America, North Mankato, MN.

Table of Contents

Where Is Montana?

Glacier National Park

Missoula

Butte

Idaho

Montana lies in the northwestern United States. It is the fourth largest state in land area. However, it is also one of the least populated. Helena is Montana's capital. It is nestled in the **foothills** of the Rocky Mountains, near the Missouri River.

Canada

North Dakota

Great Falls

Missouri River

Helena

Montana

Bozeman

Billings

South Dakota

Wyoming

Montana shares its long, straight northern border with Canada. North Dakota and South Dakota are its neighbors to the east. Wyoming creates the straight part of Montana's southern boundary. The state shares a mountainous border with Idaho to the south and west.

History

Native Americans lived in Montana for thousands of years before white explorers arrived. The discovery of gold in 1862 led to a gold rush. Miners began to settle on Native American land. In 1875, the U.S. government ordered Native Americans onto **reservations**. Montana became a state in 1889.

Did you know?

At Little Bighorn, Colonel George Custer led U.S. troops to force a band of Sioux onto reservations. Custer and more than 250 of his men were killed in the bloody battle.

Montana Timeline!

1600s: Plains Indians start to move into the Montana region from the east.

1803: The United States buys territory including much of Montana in the Louisiana Purchase.

1805-1806: Meriwether Lewis and William Clark lead explorers through Montana.

1862: Gold is discovered at Grasshopper Creek in southwestern Montana. Miners flock to the region.

1876: Cheyenne and Sioux tribes defeat U.S. troops at the Battle of the Little Bighorn.

1889: Montana becomes the forty-first state.

1902: The first *Tyrannosaurus rex* skeleton is dug up near Jordan.

1910: The wilderness area in northwestern Montana becomes Glacier National Park.

1914: Women are granted the right to vote in Montana six years before the rest of the nation.

1916: Jeannette Rankin of Missoula is the first woman elected to the U.S. House of Representatives.

Lewis and Clark

Colonel George Custer

Jeannette Rankin

The Land

Montana has two main types of land. The majestic Rocky Mountains rise in the west. The Rockies are marked by tall, rugged peaks and deep valleys. Some valleys are narrow and forested. Others are wide with dry, grassy floors. Western Montana tends to have mild winters and cool summers.

Eastern Montana is part of the **Great Plains**. This area is usually dry with hot summers and cold winters. Here, grassy plains and gently rolling hills stretch for miles. The Yellowstone River winds through Montana's colorful **badlands**.

badlands

Did you know?

The Rocky Mountains gave Montana its name. *Montana* comes from the Spanish word for "mountain."

Montana's Climate
average °F

spring
Low: 32°
High: 56°

summer
Low: 51°
High: 80°

fall
Low: 32°
High: 56°

winter
Low: 14°
High: 32°

Glacier National Park

Glacier National Park is a vast area of wilderness in northwestern Montana. It earned its name from the ancient **glaciers** that carved its stunning land features. Long ago, ice nearly one mile (1.6 kilometers) thick covered the area.

Did you know?

Montana's glaciers are melting quickly. In 1850, Glacier National Park was home to about 150 glaciers. Today, only about 25 remain. Some scientists predict all of the park's glaciers will disappear by the 2030s.

Grinnell Glacier

The park's current glaciers are much smaller than those of the past. The Blackfoot and Grinnell Glaciers are among the largest. The Blackfoot Glacier covers 0.7 square miles (1.8 square kilometers) of mountainous land. Visitors can hike past the park's glimmering lakes and soaring mountains to see Grinnell Glacier up close.

Wildlife

Montana's beautiful national parks and **nature reserves** are home to all kinds of wildlife. Graceful antelopes leap across the plains. Gray wolf packs hunt in the Rockies. Bighorn sheep also climb across the steep, rugged land. In forests, grizzly bears munch on berries while mountain lions stalk their prey.

Meadowlarks whistle in the grasslands. Bald eagles feast on trout from the Missouri River. Black and white loons dive for fish in mountain lakes. Their calls echo across the water's surface. Great blue herons wade through the water and scoop up fish with their long beaks.

bighorn sheep

loon

mountain lion

grizzly bear

Going-to-the-Sun Road

Glacier National Park welcomes about two million visitors each year. The park's Going-to-the-Sun Road is a popular 50-mile (80-kilometer) driving route. It winds through some of the park's most beautiful scenery. In the southeast, visitors to the Little Bighorn Battlefield National **Monument** can tour the sites of the historic battle.

C.M. Russell
Museum

Museum of
the Rockies

The Montana Dinosaur Trail
includes fourteen attractions
that span the state. Visitors can see ancient **fossils**,
including the bones of baby dinosaurs. Bozeman's Museum
of the Rockies is one stop on the trail. It displays the largest
Tyrannosaurus rex skull in the world.

Butte

Gold and silver first drew miners to Butte in the 1860s. Copper was discovered there in 1882. This metal became key to Butte's development. Crowds of men came to work in the mines. Soon, Butte bustled with more than 100,000 people.

Mining has since slowed in Butte. Today, only about 33,525 people live there. However, pieces of Butte's mining past live on. A maze of old mine tunnels is hidden under its streets. History fans can tour old mansions built by copper businessmen. At the World Museum of Mining, visitors can walk through an underground mine.

World Museum of Mining

fun fact

Long ago, businesses painted huge advertisements on the sides of Butte's buildings. Those companies are long gone. However, their "ghost signs" are historic treasures in Butte today.

Working

Did you know?

Montana is called the "Treasure State" because of its valuable minerals and metals.

Most Montanans have **service jobs**. They work at hospitals, schools, and banks. Others work at hotels, restaurants, and shops that serve the state's many **tourists**. Two-thirds of Montana is dedicated to farms and ranches. On the plains, farmers grow wheat, hay, and barley. Ranchers raise cattle and sheep.

Workers mine coal, oil, and natural gas from the Great Plains. Gold, copper, and talc come from the Rocky Mountains. The forests of the Rockies provide trees for lumber and paper products. The state's rushing waters produce **hydroelectricity**.

Where People Work in Montana

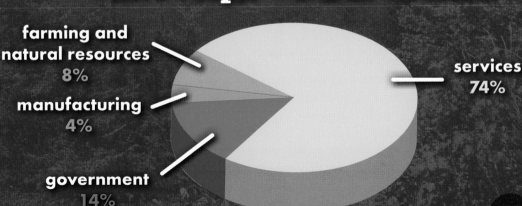

farming and natural resources
8%

manufacturing
4%

government
14%

services
74%

Playing

The Old West is still alive in Montana. Some people compete in **rodeos** or take part in square-dancing clubs. Others practice their old-time fiddling. Native Americans perform at **traditional** dance ceremonies.

Montanans also take advantage of their state's beautiful outdoors. The trails in Montana's many parks and forests are perfect for hiking and camping. Fly fishers cast their lines for trout in the Blackfoot River. In winter, people ice fish or snowshoe in the cold. Skiers speed down Rocky Mountain slopes.

fly fishing

fun fact ?

Evel Knievel was a famous daredevil from Montana. In one amazing stunt, he jumped over 50 cars on his motorcycle. He liked to brag that he had broken almost every bone in his body.

Evel Knievel

Campfire Trout

Ingredients:

4 trout fillets

Salt and pepper to taste

4 tablespoons butter, divided

1 medium green bell pepper, sliced

1 clove garlic, minced (optional)

Directions:

1. Place each fillet on a piece of aluminum foil. Season with salt and pepper. Then top each fillet with 1 tablespoon of butter, 1/4 of the green pepper, and garlic (if desired).

2. Roll the trout tightly in the foil, forming packets. Use additional foil to secure each packet to a metal toasting rod.

3. Cover the fish packets in the red-hot, smoldering coals of a campfire. Cook until the fish is done, about 7 to 10 minutes.

Makes 4 servings.

pasties

huckleberries

Montana fishers dip trout in bread crumbs and then fry it. Others wrap their catch in aluminum foil and cook it under hot coals. Pasties go back to Butte's mining days. Onions, potatoes, and meat are baked into pockets of dough. People eat the pasties by hand, sometimes with gravy on the side.

Flathead cherries come from northwestern Montana, around Flathead Lake. People bake these sweet fruits into flaky pastries to make rustic tarts. Huckleberries are another summer treat. These purple berries grow wild in the Rocky Mountains. Montanans cook them into pies, jams, and bread.

23

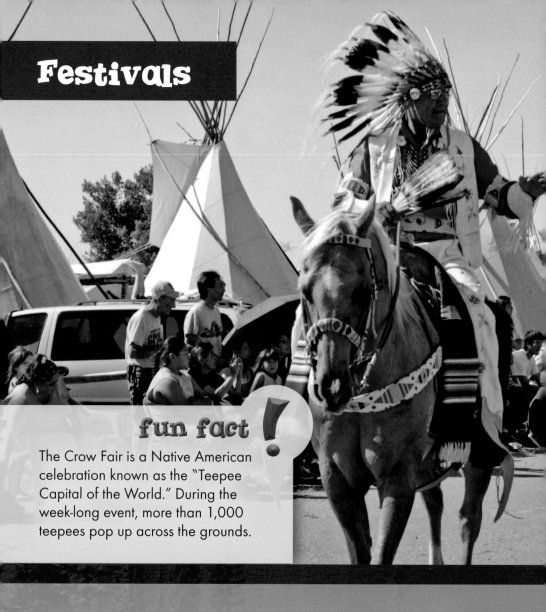

fun fact

The Crow Fair is a Native American celebration known as the "Teepee Capital of the World." During the week-long event, more than 1,000 teepees pop up across the grounds.

Each May, visitors flock to Miles City to watch rodeo events at the Bucking Horse Sale. In June, the Crow Indian Reservation hosts a **reenactment** of the Battle of the Little Bighorn. Soon after comes the Lewis and Clark Festival. It celebrates the explorers who passed through Great Falls in 1806.

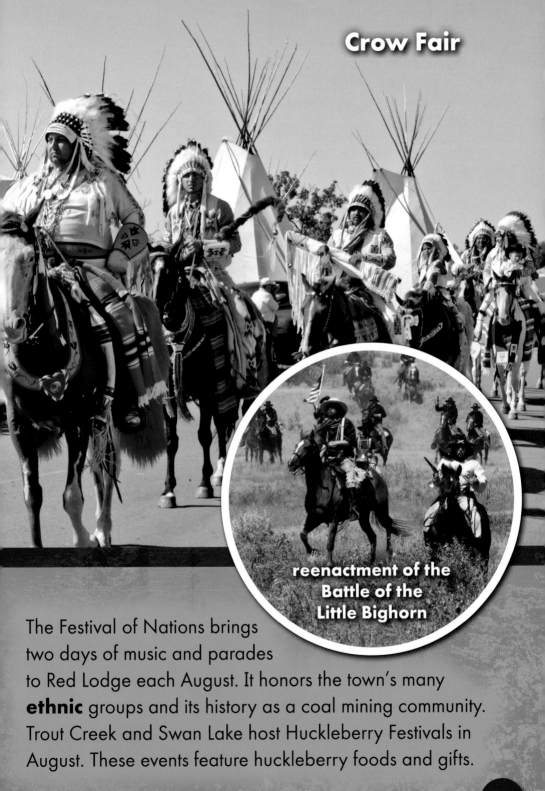

Crow Fair

reenactment of the
Battle of the
Little Bighorn

The Festival of Nations brings
two days of music and parades
to Red Lodge each August. It honors the town's many
ethnic groups and its history as a coal mining community.
Trout Creek and Swan Lake host Huckleberry Festivals in
August. These events feature huckleberry foods and gifts.

Bison

Bison, or American buffalo, were important to the **Plains Indians**. They believed bison were a gift from their god. Tribes such as the Blackfoot followed bison **migrations**. They relied on the animals for food and clothing. They even used the bones as tools and weapons.

Tens of millions of bison once roamed the plains. Their numbers greatly decreased when white settlers arrived. By 1889, only about 1,000 remained. Montanans are working to bring them back. In 2012, more than 60 bison were released on the Fort Peck Reservation. Montana's respect for its history and culture can be seen in its effort to return the majestic bison to the plains.

Fast Facts About Montana

Montana's Flag

Montana's flag is dark blue. "Montana" is written in gold across the top. Below the name is the state seal. It includes the Rocky Mountains, a river, and trees. They represent Montana's many resources. The state motto is written under a drawing of a shovel and pick. These represent Montana's mining industry.

State Flower
bitterroot

State Nicknames:	Treasure State Big Sky Country
State Motto:	*Oro y Plata*; "Gold and Silver"
Year of Statehood:	1889
Capital City:	Helena
Other Major Cities:	Billings, Missoula, Great Falls
Population:	989,415 (2010)
Area:	147,039 square miles (380,829 square kilometers); Montana is the 4th largest state.
Major Industries:	services, mining, forestry, farming
Natural Resources:	oil, natural gas, coal, gold, copper, farmland, forests
State Government:	100 representatives; 50 senators
Federal Government:	1 representative; 2 senators
Electoral Votes:	3

State Animal
grizzly bear

State Bird
western meadowlark

Glossary

badlands—dry, hilly lands that have been eroded by wind and water

ethnic—from another country or cultural background

foothills—hills at the base of a mountain

fossils—the remains of ancient plants and animals that have been preserved in stone

glaciers—massive sheets of ice that cover large areas of land

Great Plains—a region of flat or gently rolling land in the central United States; the Great Plains stretch over about one-third of the country.

hydroelectricity—power created by the force of running water

migrations—acts of traveling from one place to another, often with the seasons

monument—a structure that people build to remember important events or people

native—originally from a specific place

nature reserves—lands that are set aside to protect animal homes and keep wildlife safe

Plains Indians—Native American tribes of the Great Plains

reenactment—the performance of a historic event

reservations—areas of land the government has set aside for Native Americans

rodeos—events where people compete at tasks such as bull riding and calf roping; cowboys once completed these tasks as part of their daily work.

service jobs—jobs that perform tasks for people or businesses

tourists—people who travel to visit another place

traditional—relating to a custom, idea, or belief handed down from one generation to the next

To Learn More

AT THE LIBRARY
Aloian, Molly. *The Rocky Mountains*. New York, N.Y.: Crabtree Pub. Co., 2012.

Josephson, Judith Pinkerton. *Who Was Sitting Bull? And Other Questions About the Battle of Little Bighorn*. Minneapolis, Minn.: Lerner Classroom, 2011.

Porterfield, Jason. *Montana: Past and Present*. New York, N.Y.: Rosen Central, 2011.

ON THE WEB
Learning more about Montana is as easy as 1, 2, 3.

1. Go to www.factsurfer.com.

2. Enter "Montana" into the search box.

3. Click the "Surf" button and you will see a list of related Web sites.

With factsurfer.com, finding more information is just a click away.

Index